Incredible Adam
and a Day with Autism

We hope that you find this book from ORP Library valuable.

If this book touched you in a way that you would be willing to share, we encourage you to visit www.Amazon.com or www.BN.com and write a short review.

www.ORPLibrary.com

Writers of the Round Table Press
PO Box 511
Highland Park, IL 60035

Illustration	NATHAN LUETH
Publisher	COREY MICHAEL BLAKE
Executive Editor	KATIE GUTIERREZ
Creative Director	DAVID CHARLES COHEN
Post Production	DAVID CHARLES COHEN
Directoress of Happiness	ERIN COHEN
Director of Author Services	KRISTIN WESTBERG
Facts Keeper	MIKE WINICOUR
Front Cover Design	NATHAN LUETH, SUNNY DIMARTINO
Interior Design and Layout	SUNNY DIMARTINO
Proofreading	RITA HESS
Last Looks	SUNNY DIMARTINO
Digital Book Conversion	SUNNY DIMARTINO
Digital Publishing	SUNNY DIMARTINO

Printed in the United States of America

First Edition: July 2013
10 9 8 7 6 5 4 3 2

Library of Congress Cataloging-in-Publication Data
Krukar, Jeff
Incredible adam and a day with autism: an illustrated story inspired
by social narratives / Jeff Krukar and Chelsea McCutchin with
James G. Balestrieri and Katie Gutierrez.—1st ed. p. cm.
Print ISBN: 978-1-939418-36-4   Digital ISBN: 978-1-939418-37-1
Library of Congress Control Number: 2013944636
Number 6 in the series: The ORP Library
The ORP Library: Incredible Adam and a Day with Autism

RTC Publishing is an imprint of Writers of the Round Table, Inc.
Writers of the Round Table Press and the RTC Publishing logo
are trademarks of Writers of the Round Table, Inc.

Incredible Adam and a Day with Autism

AN ILLUSTRATED STORY INSPIRED BY SOCIAL NARRATIVES

THE ORP LIBRARY

WRITTEN BY **JEFF KRUKAR, PH.D.** · **CHELSEA McCUTCHIN**

WITH **JAMES G. BALESTRIERI** · **KATIE GUTIERREZ**

ILLUSTRATED BY **NATHAN LUETH**

Introduction

I have led Oconomowoc Residential Programs (ORP) for almost thirty years. We're a family of companies offering specialized services and care for children, adolescents, and adults with disabilities. Too often, when parents of children with disabilities try to find funding for programs like ours, they are bombarded by red tape, conflicting information, or no information at all, so they struggle blindly for years to secure an appropriate education. Meanwhile, home life, and the child's wellbeing, suffers. In cases when parents and caretakers have exhausted their options—and their hope—ORP is here to help. We felt it was time to offer parents a new, unexpected tool to fight back: stories that educate, empower, and inspire.

The original idea was to create a library of comic books that could empower families with information to reclaim their rights. We wanted to give parents and caretakers the information they need to advocate for themselves, as well as provide educators and therapists with a therapeutic tool. And, of course, we wanted to reach the children—to offer them a visual representation of their journey that would show that they aren't alone, nor are they wrong or "bad" for their differences.

What we found in the process of writing original stories for the comics is that these journeys are too long, too complex, to be contained within a standard comic. So what we are now creating is an ORP library of disabilities books—traditional books geared toward parents, caretakers, educators, and therapists, *and* comic books like this one that portray the world through the eyes of children with disabilities. Both styles of books share what we have learned while advocating for families over the years while also honestly highlighting their emotional journeys.

In an ideal situation, this companion children's book will be used therapeutically, to communicate directly with these amazing children, and to help support the work ORP and companies like ours are doing. These books are the best I have to offer and if they even help a handful of people the effort will have been worth it.

Sincerely,

Jim Balestrieri
CEO, Oconomowoc Residential Programs

A Note About This Book

Autism spectrum disorder is a complex syndrome that affects children in different ways. The child with autism spectrum disorder depicted in the following story struggles with significant emotional and behavioral difficulties that require a therapeutic environment. The great majority of children with autism spectrum disorder do not resemble the child shown in this story. But those who do resemble him face challenges that have made it difficult to benefit from education in the public school system. At Genesee Lake School, we strive to build relationships with the children in our care so that they learn new skills that will lead to a successful return to their home, school, and community. It is our hope that the following story will add to your own understanding of the often lonely journey experienced by families with children with these unique challenges and gifts.

THIS IS ADAM.

JUSTIN USUALLY HELPS ADAM START
THE DAY. TODAY, JUSTIN ISN'T HERE.
TIM WILL HELP ADAM INSTEAD.

ADAM DOESN'T WANT TO MAKE THE BED WITH TIM. ADAM WANTS TO MAKE THE BED WITH JUSTIN.

ADAM TAKES THE SHEET AND
THROWS IT OVER HIS SHOULDERS
LIKE A SUPERHERO.

LOOK!
YOU'RE MR. INCREDIBLE!
WE MUST MAKE THE BED
BEFORE THE EVIL ROBOTS
DESTROY IT!

TIM MAKES ADAM LAUGH. TIM PULLS THE
SHEET FROM ADAM'S SHOULDERS AND
SETS IT ON THE BED. TIM PUTS HIS HANDS
OVER ADAM'S AND SMOOTHS THE SHEETS.
THEN THEY TUCK THE CORNERS OF THE
SHEET UNDER THE MATTRESS.

WHEN THEY ARE DONE, TIM HOLDS UP HIS HAND FOR A HIGH FIVE. HOW HAPPY! THEY MADE MAKING THE BED TOGETHER FUN!

GREAT JOB!

TIM TELLS ADAM, "YOUR MOM, DAD, AND SISTER ARE COMING TO VISIT TODAY AFTER LUNCH." ADAM IS VERY HAPPY.

ADAM IS HUNGRY. IT IS TIME TO EAT BREAKFAST. HE GOES TO THE CAFETERIA WITH THE OTHERS. THE CAFETERIA IS FULL OF STUDENTS, AND IT IS VERY NOISY. ADAM DOESN'T LIKE THE SOUNDS; THEY ARE TOO LOUD. ADAM CLAPS HIS HANDS TO HIS EARS AND SHUTS HIS EYES SO THE NOISE WILL GO AWAY.

TIM SEES THAT ADAM
IS NOT HAPPY.

TIM PUTS HIS HANDS ON ADAM'S SHOULDERS
AND SPEAKS INTO HIS EAR SO THAT ADAM
CAN FOCUS ON TIM'S VOICE.

I CAN SEE THAT YOU'RE UPSET. LET'S TAKE SOME DEEP BREATHS. THEN WE'LL EAT BREAKFAST.

SOON, ADAM'S HEART SLOWS DOWN AND
HE IS READY TO EAT. THE STAFF POUR
WARM SYRUP ON HIS PANCAKES, AND
HE EATS THEM.

ADAM GOES TO HIS CLASSROOM AFTER
BREAKFAST. MISS GEORGIA IS ADAM'S
TEACHER. SHE SHOWS STUDENTS
THEIR SCHEDULE. FIRST THEY READ.
THEN THEY HAVE ART. ART IS ADAM'S
FAVORITE ACTIVITY! AFTER ART, THEY
WILL GO TO LUNCH.

WHILE ADAM IS FINGER PAINTING,
HIS CLASSMATE, MAX, GETS MAD.
HE SHAKES THE TABLE WHERE
THEY ARE PAINTING. ADAM'S GREEN
PAINT SPILLS ON HIS PAPER.

ADAM SLAPS THE TABLE WITH HIS
HANDS. PAINT SPATTERS ALL OVER.
HE GETS MORE MAD.

MISS GEORGIA SHOWS HIM THE SKIN
BRUSH AND THE WEIGHTED BLANKET.

HE POINTS TO THE SKIN BRUSH AND SHE BRUSHES
HIS ARMS, BACK, AND LEGS. THEN SHE PRESSES
ON HIS HEAD AND ARMS AND LEGS. HE FEELS
CALM WHEN MISS GEORGIA BRUSHES HIS SKIN
AND GIVES HIM DEEP PRESSURE.

ADAM'S HEART STOPS BEATING SO FAST, AND HE WANTS TO PAINT AGAIN. MISS GEORGIA GIVES HIM CLEAN, WHITE PAPER SO THAT HE CAN MAKE A NEW PICTURE!

ADAM LOVES TO FINGER PAINT AND ART IS HIS FAVORITE
SUBJECT. MISS GEORGIA TELLS THE STUDENTS THEY
HAVE FIVE MINUTES LEFT AND SETS THE TIMER.

THE TIMER GOES OFF, AND ADAM HAS A
HARD TIME CHANGING TO A DIFFERENT
ACTIVITY. HE FEELS ANGRY. IT FEELS LIKE
STORM CLOUDS ARE BUILDING IN HIS CHEST.

MISS GEORGIA POINTS TO THE SCHEDULE ON
THE WALL AND TELLS THE STUDENTS IT IS
ALMOST TIME FOR LUNCH. ADAM FEELS
HUNGRY. MISS GEORGIA WALKS WITH ADAM TO
THE BATHROOM AND HE WASHES HIS HANDS.

IN THE CAFETERIA, ADAM SEES WHAT'S FOR LUNCH. THERE IS NO SPAGHETTI TODAY.

HE FEELS ANGRY ABOUT THE SANDWICHES FOR LUNCH TODAY. HE FEELS ANGRY THAT MAX SPILLED HIS PAINT. HE FEELS ANGRY THAT JUSTIN WAS NOT HERE TODAY.

SUDDENLY, HE FALLS TO THE FLOOR,
SCREAMING, CRYING, AND HITTING HIS
HEAD.

TIM SITS DOWN ON THE FLOOR WITH ADAM.
HE HOLDS HIM TIGHT, APPLYING DEEP
PRESSURE WITH HIS ARMS. ADAM FEELS
CALMER. TIM KEEPS HOLDING HIM, AND THE
STORM CLOUDS START TO CLEAR.

ADAM BREATHES DEEPLY AND FEELS CALMER. HE
STANDS UP TO GET IN LINE FOR LUNCH. AT THE TABLE,
ADAM EATS THE GRILLED CHEESE SANDWICH AND AN
APPLE. IT'S OKAY.

AFTER LUNCH, ADAM GOES BACK TO THE
CLASSROOM. MISS GEORGIA REVIEWS THE
SCHEDULE FOR THE AFTERNOON.

THE WEATHER IS COLD, AND SNOW AND SLEET
ARE FALLING VERY HARD. NOW ADAM CAN'T GO
SWING ON THE PLAYGROUND.

ADAM GOES TO THE WINDOW AND TRIES TO
BREAK THE WINDOW WITH HIS FIST. HE WANTS
TO GO OUTSIDE.

HE IS VERY ANGRY. TIM COMES TO ADAM AND
MOVES HIS HANDS DOWN FOR SAFETY.

MISS GEORGIA SAYS, "I CAN SEE YOU'RE UPSET. YOU CAN USE YOUR BODY SOCK, GET DEEP PRESSURE, OR GO TO THE SENSORY ROOM."

HE POINTS TO THE BODY SOCK, AND
WHEN MISS GEORGIA WRAPS HIM UP, HE
FEELS HIS HEARTBEAT SLOW DOWN.

AFTER TWENTY MINUTES IN THE
BODY SOCK, HE FEELS CALM AGAIN.
HOW HAPPY. HOW HAPPY!

MISS GEORGIA TAKES ADAM TO THE INDOOR PLAYGROUND. HE RUNS TO THE SWING, SO EXCITED, BUT MARSHA IS ALREADY SWINGING.

ADAM IS MAD! IT WAS HIS TURN TO SWING!
HE STOMPS HIS FEET, MAKING HIMSELF BIG
SO THAT MARSHA WILL GET OFF HIS SWING!

MISS GEORGIA ROLLS THE THERAPY BALL TO ADAM.

IT'S MARSHA'S TURN NOW. FIRST, WE WILL ROLL THE THERAPY BALL. THEN YOU WILL SWING.

MARSHA IS OFF THE SWING AND MISS
GEORGIA SAYS IT'S NOW ADAM'S TURN.

SHE PUSHES LEFT AND RIGHT, BACK AND
FORTH. "MORE!" HE SAYS.

SHE PUSHES HIM MORE.

ADAM'S LAUGH ECHOES IN THE
SENSORY ROOM.

ADAM'S MOM, DAD, AND SISTER, SHANNON, ARE WAITING FOR ADAM AFTER SCHOOL!

HE IS SO HAPPY AND EXCITED TO SEE THEM. THEY ALL TAKE TURNS HUGGING ADAM, AND HE TRIES HARD TO STAND STILL TO LET THEM.

ADAM IS EXCITED TO SWING. MOM ZIPS UP HIS COAT AND HE PUTS ON HIS MITTENS. THEY GO OUTSIDE. HE CAN SEE HIS BREATH.

ADAM HOPS UP ON THE SWING,
WHERE DAD PUSHES HIM. HE WANTS
TO GO WAY UP TO THE TREES.

MORE!

HIS FAMILY LAUGHS AND SMILES WHEN
HE TELLS THEM WHAT HE WANTS. IT
MAKES THEM FEEL HAPPY.

WHEN SWINGING TIME IS OVER, MOM, DAD, AND SISTER ALL GIVE ADAM HUGS. HE WRAPS HIS ARMS AROUND THEM, TOO.

NOW IT IS BEDTIME. ADAM IS
BACK IN HIS ROOM WITH CALVIN.

FIRST, WE'RE GOING TO TAKE A SHOWER. THEN WE ARE GOING TO BRUSH YOUR TEETH.

ADAM FOLLOWS CALVIN DOWN THE HALLWAY
TO THE BATHROOM. THE WARM WATER AND
SOAP FEEL NICE ON HIS SKIN.

ADAM BRUSHES HIS TEETH AND SEES
THE SUDS ON HIS FACE IN THE MIRROR.
HOW SILLY HE LOOKS.

ADAM PUTS ON HIS PAJAMAS, AND CALVIN
AND ADAM GO BACK TO HIS BEDROOM.

ADAM IS VERY SLEEPY. CALVIN
HELPS ADAM GET INTO HIS BED.

CALVIN TURNS TO ADAM JUST BEFORE TURNING OUT THE LIGHT.

"GOODNIGHT, MR. INCREDIBLE."

ADAM SMILES. HOW HAPPY.

How These Books Were Created

The ORP Library of disabilities books is the result of heartfelt collaboration between numerous people: the staff of ORP, including the CEO, executive director, psychologists, clinical coordinators, teachers, and more; the families of children with disabilities served by ORP, including some of the children themselves; and the Round Table Companies (RTC) storytelling team. To create these books, RTC conducted dozens of intensive, intimate interviews over a period of months and performed independent research in order to truthfully and accurately depict the lives of these families. We are grateful to all those who donated their time in support of this message, generously sharing their experience, wisdom, and—most importantly—their stories so that the books will ring true. While each story is fictional and not based on any one family or child, we could not have envisioned the world through their eyes without the access we were so lovingly given. It is our hope that in reading this uniquely personal book, you felt the spirit of everyone who contributed to its creation.

Acknowledgments

The authors would like to thank the following team members at Genesee Lake School and ORP who generously lent their time and expertise to this book: clinical coordinator Eric Fleischmann, occupational therapists Tracy Hoffman and Gus Ludwig, ICARE program coordinator Jim Lynch, speech and language pathologist Cheryl Norstrem, program supervisors Tony Pierson and Dan Staffin, and special education teacher Emily Richter. Your passion, experience, and wisdom make this book an invaluable tool for other educators, families, and therapists. Thank you for your enthusiastic contributions to this project.

We would also like to extend our heartfelt gratitude to the families who shared their journeys with us. To the Sam Haas family; to Amy, David, Emily, and Andrew Metz; to Linda Rose and her little angel, Hannah; and to Bridgitt and Kevin Montijo, parents of Kyle—thank you for letting us into your worlds, for sharing with us so openly your times of worry, fear, desperation, determination, love, and hope. The courage, ferocity, and love with which you shepherd your children through their lives is nothing short of heroic. You are the reason this book exists.

And to readers of *Incredible Adam*—the parents committed to helping their children, the educators who teach those children skills needed for greater independence, the therapists who shine a light on what can be a frighteningly mysterious road, and the schools and counties that make difficult financial decisions to benefit these children: thank you. Your work is miraculous.

Resources

American Psychiatric Association. *Diagnostic and Statistical Manual of Mental Disorders, Fourth Edition, Text Revision*. Washington, DC: American Psychiatric Association, 2000.

Ayres, A. Jean. *Sensory Integration and the Child, 25th Anniversary Edition: Understanding Hidden Sensory Challenges*. Los Angeles, CA: Western Psychological Services, 2005.

Baker, Jed. *No More Meltdowns: Positive Strategies for Managing and Preventing Out-of-Control Behavior*. Arlington, TX: Future Horizons, 2008.

Biel, Lindsey, and Peske, Nancy. *Raising a Sensory Smart Child: The Definitive Handbook for Helping Your Child With Sensory Processing Issues*. New York, NY: Penguin Group, 2009.

Frost, Lori, and Bondy, Andy. *The Picture Exchange Communication System Training Manual*. Cherry Hill, NJ: Pyramid Educational Consultants, Inc., 2002.

Gray, Carol. *The New Social Story Book: Illustrated Edition*. Arlington, TX: Future Horizons, 2000.

Gray, Carol, and White, Abbie Leigh. *My Social Stories Book*. London: Jessica Kingsley Publishers, 2002.

Greenspan, Stanley, and Wieder, Serena. *The Child with Special Needs: Encouraging Intellectual and Emotional Growth*. Cambridge, MA: Da Capo Press, 1998.

Greenspan, Stanley, and Wieder, Serena. *Engaging Autism: Using the Floortime Approach to Help Children Relate, Communicate, and Think*. Cambridge, MA: Da Capo Press, 2006.

Hodgdon, Linda. *Visual Strategies for Improving Communication*. Troy, MI: Quirk Roberts Publishing, 1995.

Reed, Penny. *Designing Environments for Successful Kids: A Resource Manual*. Oshkosh, WI: Wisconsin Assistive Technology Initiative, 2003.

"Autism Internet Modules," *http://www.autisminternetmodules.org*.

"IDEA – Building the Legacy: IDEA 2004," *http://idea.ed.gov*.

"Interdisciplinary Council on Developmental and Learning Disorders," *http://www.icdl.com*.

"National Professional Development Center on Autism Spectrum Disorders. Evidence-Based Practice: Social Narratives," *autism pdc.fpg.unc.edu*.

Nathan Lueth

BIOGRAPHY

Nathan came into existence with a pencil in his hand, a feat that continues to confound obstetricians to this day. No one knows for sure when he started drawing or where his love of comics came from, but most experts agree that his professional career began after graduating from the Minneapolis College of Art and Design, as a caricaturist in the Mall of America. Soon he was freelance illustrating for the likes of Target, General Mills, and Stone Arch Books.

When not drawing comics for other people, Nathan draws his own super awesome fantasy webcomic, *Impure Blood*. He is proud to be a part of Round Table Companies, as he believes that comics should be for everyone, not just nerds (it should be noted that he may be trying to turn the general population into nerds). He currently resides in St. Paul, Minnesota, with two cats, a turtle, and his wife, Nadja, upon whom he performs his nerd conversion experiments.

Jeffrey D. Krukar, Ph.D.

BIOGRAPHY

Jeffrey D. Krukar, Ph.D. is a licensed psychologist and certified school psychologist with more than 20 years of experience working with children and families in a variety of settings, including community based group homes, vocational rehabilitation services, residential treatment, juvenile corrections, public schools, and private practice. He earned his Ph.D. in educational psychology, with a school psychology specialization and psychology minor, from the University of Wisconsin-Milwaukee. Dr. Krukar is a registrant of the National Register of Health Service Providers in Psychology, and is also a member of the American Psychological Association.

As the psychologist at Genesee Lake School in Oconomowoc, WI, Dr. Krukar believes it truly takes a village to raise a child—to strengthen developmental foundations in relating, communicating, and thinking—so they can successfully return to their families and communities. Dr. Krukar hopes the ORP Library of disabilities books will bring to light the stories of children and families to a world that is generally not aware of their challenges and successes, as well as offer a sense of hope to those currently on this journey. His deepest hope is that some of the concepts in these books resonate with parents and professionals working with kids with disabilities, and offer possibilities that will help kids achieve their maximum potential and life enjoyment.

Chelsea McCutchin

BIOGRAPHY

Chelsea McCutchin believes that the transformative power of story is what has bound us together as humanity for ages. She is blessed to work with Round Table Companies, Inc. as a staff editor. She is humbled to be the vessel relaying the challenges and triumphs of families of children with autism spectrum disorder. Chelsea studied English and creative writing at the University of Texas at Austin, and when she isn't writing can be found with her supportive husband, Matt, and their amazing son, Jackson, in her home state of Florida.

James G. Balestrieri

BIOGRAPHY

James G. Balestrieri is currently the CEO of Oconomowoc Residential Programs, Inc. (ORP). He has worked in the human services field for 40 years, holding positions that run the gamut to include assistant maintenance, assistant cook, direct care worker, teacher's aide, summer camp counselor, bookkeeper, business administrator, marketing director, CFO, and CEO. Jim graduated from Marquette University with a B.S. in Business Administration (1977) and a Master's in Business Administration with an emphasis in Marketing (1988). He is also a Certified Public Accountant (Wisconsin—1982). Jim has a passion for creatively addressing the needs of those with impairments by managing the inherent stress among funding, programming, and profitability. He believes that those with a disability enjoy rights and protections that were created by the hard-fought efforts of those who came before them; that the Civil Rights movement is not just for minority groups; and that people with disabilities have a right to find their place in the world and to achieve their maximum potential as individuals. For more information, see *www.orp.com*.

Katie Gutierrez

BIOGRAPHY

Katie Gutierrez believes that a well-told story can transcend what a reader "knows" to be real about the world—and thus change the world for that reader. In every form, story is transformative, and Katie is proud to spend her days immersed in it as executive editor for Round Table Companies, Inc.

Since 2007, Katie has edited approximately 50 books and co-written six—including *Meltdown* and *An Unlikely Trust*, two of the ORP Library of disabilities books. She has been humbled by the stories she has heard and hopes these books will help guide families on their often-lonely journeys, connecting them with resources and support. She also hopes they will give the general population a glimpse into the Herculean jobs taken on so fiercely by parents, doctors, therapists, educators, and others who live with, work with, and love children like Adam.

Katie holds a BA in English and philosophy from Southwestern University and an MFA in fiction from Texas State University. She has contributed to or been profiled in publications including *Forbes*, *Entrepreneur* magazine, *People* magazine, *Hispanic Executive Quarterly*, and *Narrative* magazine. She can't believe she's lucky enough to do what she loves every day.

About ORP

Oconomowoc Residential Programs, Inc. is an employee-owned family of companies whose mission is to make a difference in the lives of people with disabilities. Our dedicated staff of 2,000 employee owners provides quality services and professional care to more than 1,700 children, adolescents, and adults with special needs. ORP provides a continuum of care, including residential therapeutic education, community-based residential services, support services, respite care, treatment programs, and day services. The individuals in our care include people with developmental disabilities, physical disabilities, and intellectual disabilities. **Our guiding principle is passion:** a passion for the people we serve and for the work we do. For a comprehensive look at our programs and people, please visit *www.orp.com*.

ORP offers two residential therapeutic education programs and one alternative day school among its array of services. These programs offer developmentally appropriate education and treatment for children, adolescents, and young adults in settings specially attuned to their needs. We provide special programs for students with specific academic and social issues relative to a wide range of disabilities, including autistic disorder, Asperger's disorder, mental retardation, anxiety disorders, depression, bipolar disorder, reactive attachment disorder, attention deficit disorder, Prader-Willi Syndrome, and other disabilities.

Genesee Lake School is a nationally recognized provider of comprehensive residential treatment, educational, and vocational services for children, adolescents, and young adults with emotional, mental health, neurological, or developmental disabilities. GLS has specific expertise in Autism Spectrum Disorders, anxiety and mood disorders, and behavioral disorders. We provide an individualized, person-centered, integrated team approach, which emphasizes positive behavioral support, therapeutic relationships, and developmentally appropriate practices. Our goal is to assist each individual to acquire skills to live, learn, and succeed in a community-based, less restrictive environment. GLS is particularly known for its high quality educational services for residential and day school students.

> Genesee Lake School / Admissions Director
> 36100 Genesee Lake Road
> Oconomowoc, WI 53066
> 262-569-5510
> *http://www.geneseelakeschool.com*

T.C. Harris School is located in an attractive setting in Lafayette, Indiana. T.C. Harris teaches skills to last a lifetime, through a full therapeutic program as well as day school and other services.

> T.C. Harris School / Admissions Director
> 3700 Rome Drive
> Lafayette, IN 47905
> 765-448-4220
> *http://tcharrisschool.com*

The Richardson School is a day school in West Allis, Wisconsin that provides an effective, positive alternative education environment serving children from Milwaukee and the surrounding communities.

> The Richardson School / Director
> 6753 West Roger Street
> West Allis, WI 53219
> 414-540-8500
> *http://www.richardsonschool.com*

AUTISM SPECTRUM DISORDER

Mr. Incredible shares the fictional story of Adam, a boy diagnosed with autistic disorder. On Adam's first birthday, his mother recognizes that something is different about him: he recoils from the touch of his family, preferring to accept physical contact only in the cool water of the family's pool. As Adam grows older, he avoids eye contact, is largely nonverbal, and has very specific ways of getting through the day; when those habits are disrupted, intense meltdowns and self-harmful behavior follow. From seeking a diagnosis to advocating for special education services, from keeping Adam safe to discovering his strengths, his family becomes his biggest champion. The journey to realizing Adam's potential isn't easy, but with hope, love, and the right tools and teammates, they find that Adam truly is *Mr. Incredible*. The companion comic in this series, inspired by social stories, offers an innovative, dynamic way to guide children—and parents, educators, and caregivers—through some of the daily struggles experienced by those with autism.

MR. INCREDIBLE
A STORY ABOUT AUTISM,
OVERCOMING CHALLENGING
BEHAVIOR, AND A FAMILY'S FIGHT
FOR SPECIAL EDUCATION RIGHTS

INCREDIBLE ADAM
AND A DAY WITH AUTISM
AN ILLUSTRATED STORY
INSPIRED BY SOCIAL NARRATIVES

REACTIVE ATTACHMENT DISORDER

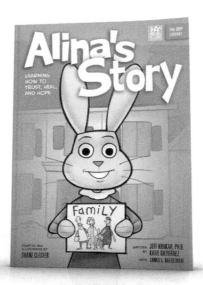

AN UNLIKELY TRUST
ALINA'S STORY OF ADOPTION, COMPLEX TRAUMA, HEALING, AND HOPE

ALINA'S STORY
LEARNING HOW TO TRUST, HEAL, AND HOPE

An Unlikely Trust: Alina's Story of Adoption, Complex Trauma, Healing, and Hope, and its companion children's book, *Alina's Story*, share the journey of Alina, a young girl adopted from Russia. After living in an orphanage during her early life, Alina is unequipped to cope with the complexities of the outside world. She has a deep mistrust of others and finds it difficult to talk about her feelings. When she is frightened, overwhelmed, or confused, she lashes out in rages that scare her family. Alina's parents know she needs help and work endlessly to find it for her, eventually discovering a special school that will teach Alina new skills. Slowly, Alina gets better at expressing her feelings and solving problems. For the first time in her life, she realizes she is truly safe and loved . . . and capable of loving in return.

ASPERGER'S DISORDER

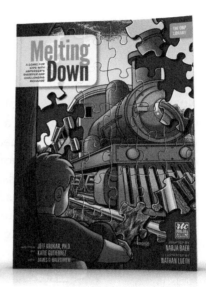

MELTDOWN
ASPERGER'S DISORDER, CHALLENGING BEHAVIOR, AND A FAMILY'S JOURNEY TOWARD HOPE

MELTING DOWN
A COMIC FOR KIDS WITH ASPERGER'S DISORDER AND CHALLENGING BEHAVIOR

Meltdown and its companion comic book, *Melting Down*, are both based on the fictional story of Benjamin, a boy diagnosed with Asperger's disorder and additional challenging behavior. From the time Benjamin is a toddler, he and his parents know he is different: he doesn't play with his sister, refuses to make eye contact, and doesn't communicate well with others. And his tantrums are not like normal tantrums; they're meltdowns that will eventually make regular schooling—and day-to-day life—impossible. Both the prose book, intended for parents, educators, and mental health professionals, and the comic for the kids themselves demonstrate that the journey toward hope isn't simple . . . but with the right tools and teammates, it's possible.

BULLYING

Nearly one third of all school children face physical, verbal, cyber, and social bullying on a regular basis. For years, educators and parents have searched for ways to end bullying, but as that behavior becomes more sophisticated, it's harder to recognize and to stop. In *Classroom Heroes* and its companion comic book, Jason is a quiet, socially awkward seventh grade boy who has long suffered bullying in silence. While Jason's parents notice him becoming angrier and more withdrawn, they don't realize the scope of the problem until one bully takes it too far—and one teacher acts on her determination to stop it. Both *Classroom Heroes* and its companion comic recognize that in order to stop bullying, we must change our mindset. We must enlist not only parents and educators but the children themselves to create a community that simply does not tolerate bullying. Jason's story demonstrates both the heartbreaking effects of bullying and the simple yet profound strategies to end it, one student at a time.

CLASSROOM HEROES

ONE CHILD'S STRUGGLE
WITH BULLYING AND
A TEACHER'S MISSION TO
CHANGE SCHOOL CULTURE

CLASSROOM HEROES

COMPANION CHILDREN'S BOOK

FAMILY SUPPORT

CHASING HOPE
YOUR COMPASS FOR A NEW NORMAL
NAVIGATING THE WORLD OF THE SPECIAL NEEDS CHILD

Schuyler Walker was just four years old when he was diagnosed with autism, bipolar disorder, and ADHD. In 2004, childhood mental illness was rarely talked about or understood. With knowledge and resources scarce, Schuyler's mom, Christine, navigated a lonely maze to determine what treatments, medications, and therapies could benefit her son. In the ten years since his diagnosis, Christine has often wished she had a "how to" guide that would provide the real mom-to-mom information she needed to survive the day and, in the end, help her family navigate the maze with knowledge, humor, grace, and love. Christine may not have had a manual at the beginning of her journey, but she hopes this book will serve as yours.

Also look for books on Prader-Willi Syndrome and children and psychotropic medications coming soon!

CPSIA information can be obtained at www.ICGtesting.com
Printed in the USA
BVOW11s1228010414

349302BV00003B/3/P